Everything You Need to Know About

Hepatitis

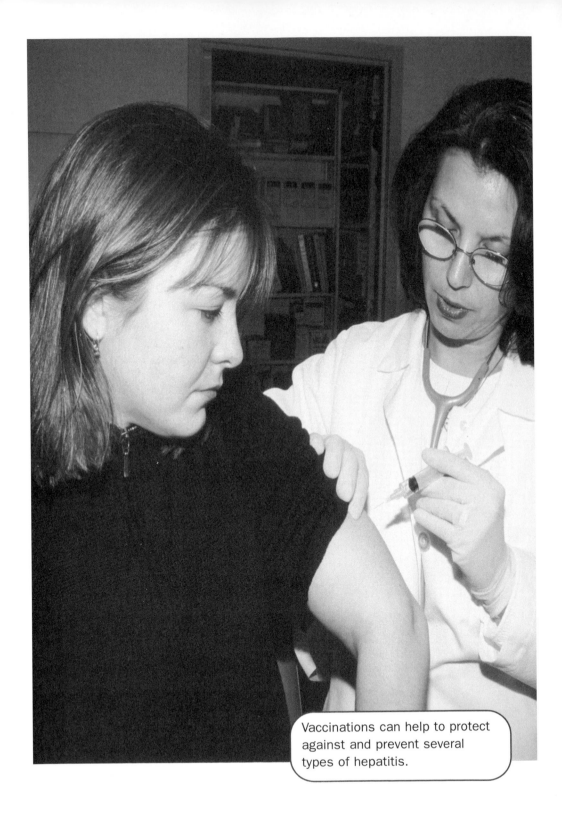

Vaccinations can help to protect against and prevent several types of hepatitis.

Everything You Need to Know About

Hepatitis

Virginia Aronson

Rosen Publishing Group, Inc.
New York

Many thanks to Ed Goodstein, R.D., M.S., for his candid discussions about hep, and to the Hepatitis Foundation International and the Hepatitis B Foundation for providing resource information.

Published in 2000 by The Rosen Publishing Group, Inc.
29 East 21st Street, New York, NY 10010

Cataloging-in-Publication Data

Aronson, Virginia.
    Everything you need to know about hepatitis/ Virginia Aronson.
       p.   cm. — (The need to know library)
    Includes bibliographical references and index.
    Summary: Explains what hepatitis is, how it is diagnosed and treated, and its effect on a person's life.
    ISBN 0-8239-3100-5
    1. Hepatitis— Juvenile literature.   [1. Hepatitis
  2. Diseases] I. Title II. Series
616.3'623—dc21

Manufactured in the United States of America

Contents

Family members with hepatitis need a lot of love and support.

Introduction

When Jenna was eighteen, her mother was diagnosed with hepatitis B. All of her siblings tested negative, but Jenna had caught the virus from her mother. At a family meeting held in the doctor's office, Jenna was asked to prepare a list of her sexual partners—each of whom she would have to inform about her disease and their risk of exposure to it. Jenna was mortified, and she felt as if future dating would be out of the question.

Everyone knows about AIDS these days, about how dangerous it is and how you can contract the disease. Few people recognize the more common and more contagious threat posed by another killer disease: hepatitis. Yet one form of hepatitis—hepatitis B—is actually 100 times more contagious than the AIDS virus, and adolescents and young adults have the greatest risk of contracting it.

Although it does not kill in every case, hepatitis is the eighth leading cause of death in the world today. A growing global problem, "hep" kills an estimated 1.2 million people every year. Millions more are sickened by this dangerous illness, while others become chronic carriers: They suffer no symptoms, but the deadly virus is present in their bodies and can be passed on to others.

Hep afflicts people of all ages and both sexes living in most parts of the world. By definition, hepatitis is an inflammation of the liver that may be due to various causes—including a number of viruses called hepatitis A, B, C, D, and E. The symptoms include jaundice, which is a yellowing of the whites of the eyes and the skin, plus nausea and vomiting, stomach pain, fever, extreme fatigue, muscle and joint pain.

The disease can be contracted from eating contaminated food or drinking contaminated water, which will cause hepatitis A or E. Hepatitis B, C, and D are transmitted the way the AIDS virus is spread: by contaminated blood in needles shared by drug users, by sexual activity with infected partners, and by infected mothers who pass it to their babies.

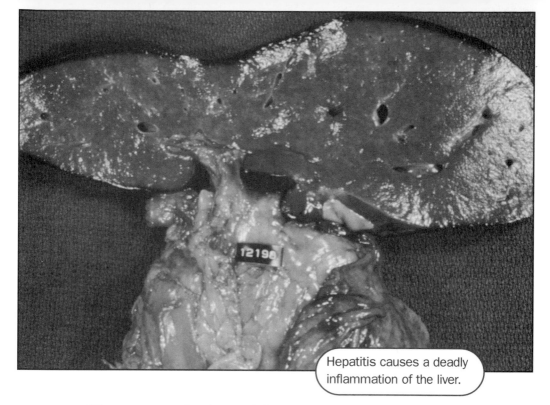

Hepatitis causes a deadly inflammation of the liver.

Treatments for hepatitis are limited and not always successful. Fortunately, most people are able to recover from the disease on their own. People with hepatitis are instructed to rest while their symptoms are treated to make them feel more comfortable. Sometimes drugs are used to boost their immune system, which helps to strengthen the body's ability to fight off the virus. In the most serious cases, liver transplants may be necessary when this essential organ is damaged beyond repair.

Vaccines are now available for hepatitis A and B. There are ways you can protect yourself from the other forms of the disease as well. You need to be aware, and to make wise choices. In most cases, you will be able to stay healthy.

This book will tell you the facts you need to know about hepatitis. Reading the chapters that follow will help you to learn how you can recognize the symptoms and receive early treatment for the various forms of hep. And you can discover how to reduce your risk of contracting this very common, highly contagious, and serious disease.

Chapter One

The ABCs of Hepatitis

In 1991, Naomi Judd and her daughter Wynonna were living out the American dream. Their country music duo, The Judds, had been voted the "Duet of the Year" for eight years, and they were country music's top-selling female performers. In the U.S. alone, the Judds had sold over 15 million albums and brought home six Grammys. They were rich, famous, and well-loved by millions of fans all over the world.

But Naomi was, at age forty-five, suffering from chronic active hepatitis. She gave what was to be her last concert in December 1991, then retired from the public eye. Despite her fear of performing alone, Wynonna was determined to carry on and, with her mother's support and blessings, she continued to wow audiences as a solo act.

Country singer Naomi Judd is a hepatitis survivor.

When Naomi was diagnosed with the disease in 1990, her doctors informed her that she would only survive for two years. They also admitted that, because she was suffering from hepatitis C, there was little they could do. "This was a death knell," Naomi recalls now.

The gifted singer grew increasingly tired and weak, eventually becoming deathly ill. "I was in a wheelchair, in the fetal position in a dark room," Naomi remembers about the lowest point of her illness. "Since my liver was compromised, it felt as if I was being poisoned from within. I couldn't finish sentences. I'd forget where I was. Who I was."

Before her career as a country singer took off in 1983, Naomi Judd was a single mother (the actress Ashley Judd is her youngest) who supported her family by working as a registered nurse. It is likely that she contracted the hepatitis C virus while practicing at various Nashville-area hospitals, possibly from an accidental puncture with a contaminated needle. For years, the virus caused no obvious symptoms, and Naomi was unaware that anything was wrong with her health.

What Is Hepatitis?

Hepatitis is an inflammation or infection of the liver, an essential organ in your body. A large gland located in the upper right portion of the abdomen, your liver

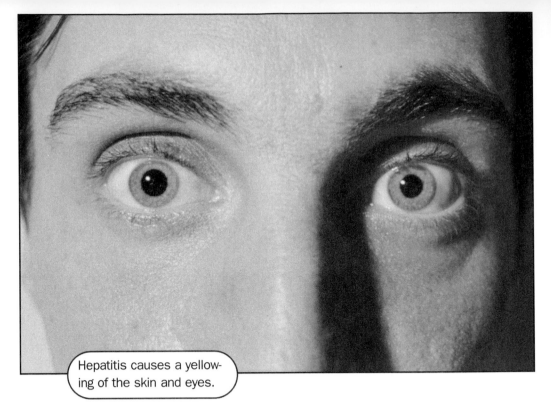

Hepatitis causes a yellowing of the skin and eyes.

has many important functions. It is involved in the digestion of food, for one, and helps to metabolize and detoxify, or deactivate, harmful substances in the bloodstream—including alcohol and drugs.

Hepatitis has been around since ancient times, the strangely horrible appearance of yellowed skin and eyes noted by doctors over the centuries. The disease has occurred around the world in epidemics, that is, in outbreaks affecting large numbers of people. Typically, hepatitis epidemics have occurred during wartime. It was during World War II that medical researchers finally realized the illness was being spread through contact with infected blood.

Since the mid-1960s, hepatitis has become a major health problem the world over and is now a leading cause of death. Also, because the disease can be mild and without symptoms, many people who have hepatitis do not know that they have been infected by the virus. Unaware, they spread the disease to others. By some estimates, 500 million people are carriers of hep.

The Silent Threat

Hepatitis is a killer disease, but few people die from it right away. Usually, an infected person will suffer from mild, flu-like symptoms at first, developing the more serious consequences years later. Thus, you might contract the disease when you're in your teens, but not know it until you are middle-aged.

This is not a good reason to ignore the threat posed by hep. But the long time between contact with the hepatitis virus and the appearance of debilitating symptoms may explain why most people know next to nothing about hep.

Few people understand that we are all at risk for developing hep. Most Americans believe that it is a disease that exists in other places, poor areas of the world where the sanitation is not good. Many think that only intravenous (or IV) drug users, people who inject drugs into their bloodstreams, are at risk. Some people mistakenly believe that the disease risk is limited to those receiving blood transfusions. That is not the case for hep.

In reality, hep is an equal opportunity affliction: Anyone can catch it almost anywhere in the world and at any age. Hepatitis has spread widely across the globe over the past thirty to forty years. Public awareness is just beginning to catch up.

Causes of Hep

There are a number of different causes for nonviral (or "toxic") hepatitis, including alcohol abuse, exposure to dangerous chemicals, use of drugs, and other lifestyle factors. Thus, alcoholics may develop hep, as can workers exposed to toxic chemicals in the workplace. A chemical once widely used in dry cleaning, carbon tetrachloride, damaged the livers of many people in the industry before the toxicity was discovered. When taken in large quantities over a long period, acetaminophen (brand name Tylenol), disulfiram (used to treat alcoholism), and isoniazid (used to treat tuberculosis) have been known to cause hepatitis. Chronic drug abuse is very hard on the liver and can also result in hepatitis.

However, the current significant global increase in the incidence of hepatitis is largely attributed to the spread of a number of viruses: hepatitis A (HAV), hepatitis B (HBV), hepatitis C (HCV), hepatitis D (HDV), and hepatitis E (HEV). Researchers have also identified hepatitis F (HFV), and hepatitis G (HGV) and its variants (HGBV).

Each of these viruses is different, but they have one

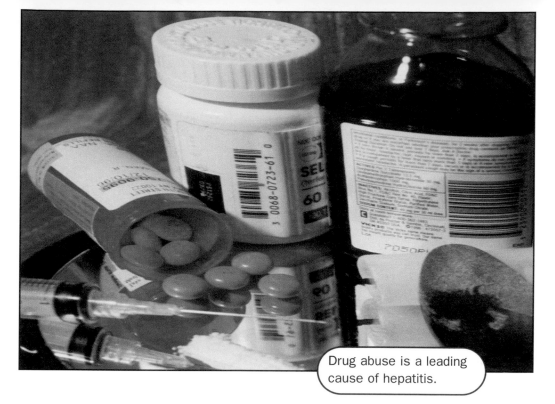

Drug abuse is a leading cause of hepatitis.

thing in common. Hep viruses take aim at the liver, where they can do the most damage.

Hepatitis A used to be called infectious hepatitis, hepatitis B was known as serum (or blood) hepatitis, and hepatitis C was referred to as non-A, non-B hepatitis. Hepatitis D can only infect the cells of the body which are already infected with HBV, so HDV makes cases of HBV worse. Hepatitis E used to be known as epidemic non-A, non-B hepatitis. A relatively new virus, researchers believe it may be less than 100 years old. Scientists have only recently discovered what they think are several more hep viruses—HGV and the HGBVs— and many believe other undiscovered hep viruses also exist. (Little is known about HFV, with only one confirmed case of hepatitis F in Canada to date.)

What You Need to Know

This may seem like a confusing alphabet soup of viruses for you to attempt to comprehend! Fortunately, the most important things to learn about hep are the easiest facts to understand: What behaviors can you change in order to reduce your risk of contracting hepatitis A, B, C, D, E, and the rest? And, if you find out that you have hep, what exactly can you do about it?

After being told by a medical specialist that she was probably suffering from a chronic case of hepatitis, that is, a form of the virus that would not be cured but would worsen with time, Naomi Judd left the doctor's office in shock. Later, depression set in. But one day, after yet another discouraging visit to the doctor's office, the popular singer made a brave and, it turns out, life-saving decision. As they drove home in their big white limo, Naomi turned to Wynonna. "I promised her and myself, 'I'm going to beat this thing by becoming involved in healing myself!'" she said.

Hepatitis is a frightening illness mainly because it is so widely misunderstood. Although hep can prove fatal, most people who have the illness do recover—and largely on their own. Armed with the facts about hepatitis A through G, you will feel less fearful—and you may make wiser choices.

It may be best to begin at the beginning, with hepatitis A.

Talk to a doctor to get the facts about hepatitis.

Chapter Two

Hepatitis A and E

Hepatitis A and E are short-term threats to health, and most people who contract these viruses recover completely in a matter of weeks. Once you have been infected with either HAV or HEV, your body develops an immunity to the virus, protecting you from future infections. However, the symptoms of the virus can be very unpleasant and uncomfortable, and the disease can prove fatal in a small percentage of cases. Prevention is relatively simple and is always the wisest course of action.

Hep Invader A

Hepatitis A may be the best known form of hep, and many people know that you can contract the illness after eating "bad" food. But this is only part of the story. Hepatitis A is actually caused by a virus that survives in human feces, so HAV is spread through sewage-contaminated food, water, or by those who fail to wash their hands properly after handling fecal matter, such as day care center employees or babysitters who change soiled diapers. The virus is transmitted easily, so it can be readily passed on to household members, friends, and neighbors.

Hep A is contracted by an estimated 150,000 Americans every year, although many cases go unreported. Outbreaks are often traced to infected food handlers in restaurants, who spread the virus to diners, and to workers in child care centers who pass on the virus to their young clients and their families.

Outbreaks also occur when people consume infected foodstuffs that come from or have been irrigated with feces-contaminated water. Raw and undercooked shellfish derived from water contaminated by raw sewage can infect consumers with hepatitis A. Fruits and vegetables irrigated with sewage-contaminated water can also be a source of the HAV infection.

Mark was out celebrating with a bunch of his high school buds while on vacation in the Bahamas. It was his nineteenth birthday, and he had a wad of cash in his pocket—a gift from his parents, who were back at home in Michigan. At the local seafood shack, Mark ordered a dozen oysters on the half-shell, which he ate himself, since his friends were dining on conch fritters and crab cakes.

The rest of the vacation flew by, and Mark returned home tanned and refreshed. He soon came down with what he thought to be a bad case of the flu, as he was suffering from severe nausea, diarrhea, and vomiting. But when he was still feeling sick several weeks later, Mark wondered whether he had picked up something worse on his trip.

Mark's mother insisted on a visit to the family physician after Mark's appetite continued to be poor and his weight began to drop. The doctor suspected and ran a blood test for hepatitis, later informing Mark that he had indeed picked up something serious: hepatitis A, most likely in the raw seafood he had eaten while on vacation.

Fortunately, all of the symptoms disappeared after a few more weeks of rest and, as the doctor had informed Mark, there was no lingering illness once the virus had run its course. These days, Mark chooses broiled fish or other cooked seafoods when he dines out—whether away on vacation or close to home.

Raw seafood like oysters can be a source of hep A.

Preventing Hep A

People who contract HAV typically suffer from nausea, vomiting, diarrhea, appetite loss, fever, fatigue, and sometimes jaundice. The symptoms may last for several weeks or even several months. Every year, around 100 people—usually the elderly or those with underlying liver disease—die from complications resulting from the hepatitis A virus.

There is no treatment for hep A other than rest, but there is an effective vaccine. Even though HAV does not lead to chronic hepatitis or liver disease, and it does not linger in the body (so you won't become a lifelong carrier of HAV), it is contagious and it can prove to be a

Washing your hands can prevent hep infection.

debilitating illness while it lasts. The vaccine is readily available and safe, providing protection from HAV for at least twenty years.

For those at risk of HAV, vaccination may be the smart choice. Travelers to underdeveloped countries, people with chronic liver disease, and those who work in nursing or day care centers can opt for the hepatitis A vaccine and thereby avoid contracting the HAV form of hep. Health authorities also recommend that people who use intravenous drugs be vaccinated, although this means of viral transmission for hep A is rare. Sexually active gay or bisexual men who do not use condoms are considered to be at risk for HAV, and may elect to receive the vaccine for preventative reasons.

If you are exposed to hepatitis A and know it—if someone in your family is diagnosed or an outbreak occurs in a restaurant where you've recently dined—a prompt dose of immune globulin (Ig), a blood plasma substance, can prevent the onset of the virus and its symptoms. If administered within one to two weeks of exposure to the virus, before any symptoms appear, the drug can provide temporary protection from hep A.

Other methods for avoiding hepatitis A are common-sense measures anyone can take, including washing your hands after using the bathroom—and avoiding raw shellfish, such as oysters (or clams) on the half-shell. You can read more about prevention in chapter five.

Hep Invader E

Hepatitis E is not commonly found in this country, but the virus can be imported to the United States by travelers returning from other areas where it is wide-spread: Parts of Mexico, Africa, Asia, and other developing regions, where poor sanitation and over-crowding regularly coexist, report epidemics and sporadic outbreaks of hepatitis E. Thus, people who have been to these places may be at risk and can unknowingly spread the virus.

As with hepatitis A, the symptoms of HEV can make you feel pretty awful, but the disease is relatively short-lived. So far, there are no reported cases of chronic HEV infection, nor do infected people become carriers. Most people simply recover on their own after resting and letting the virus run its course. Hepatitis E is rarely fatal, but does prove extremely dangerous during pregnancy when the virus can cause liver failure, even death.

Currently, there are no blood tests to determine if you are suffering from hepatitis E, so the virus can be difficult to diagnose. There is no vaccine, nor are there any specific drugs useful in treating the virus. As with HAV, prevention seems to be the best option—which, in the case of hepatitis E, means taking care when traveling to foreign countries (more in chapter five).

Approximately one out of every 250 Americans contracts hepatitis A, and the virus tends to infect children and teens more frequently than adults. It is highly contagious, especially in the first two weeks of infection when symptoms are nonexistent.

Fortunately, HAV causes only "acute" or short-term hepatitis, not chronic liver disease. The same is true for HEV. The other hepatitis viruses, however, tend to be much more severe, the resulting illnesses long-lasting, life-changing, and, in many cases, life-threatening.

Chapter Three

Hepatitis B, C, and D

Viruses are like invisible invaders, which sneak into the body, then attack a specific target. The hepatitis viruses all head straight for the liver, where they rapidly reproduce, eventually overwhelming the healthy liver cells. In response, the immune system of the body produces antibodies, which try to fight off the invaders, attacking the infected liver cells. The result of this internal battle is an inflamed liver, which leads to all of the uncomfortable symptoms of hepatitis.

Given adequate time and rest, the body's immune system will usually succeed in fighting off the viral invaders, and the liver will heal itself. Since the liver is the organ responsible for processing drugs, however, most medications cannot be taken by someone with hepatitis. The ailing liver would not be capable of handling the medication (nor can it process alcohol, caffeine, or recreational drugs like marijuana) until recovery is complete. With hepatitis, you have to just let the body take care of its own internal battle—and hope that your immune system will be able to win out over the hep virus.

If you contract hepatitis A or E, a full recovery is almost always attained. With hepatitis B, C, and D, however, healing can be more difficult, even impossible, to achieve.

Hep Invader B

Hepatitis B is the most common form of the disease in this country, with around 200,000 new cases diagnosed each year. Health authorities estimate that one out of every twenty people in the U.S. will contract hep B. The symptoms of HBV can be severe, but many people have no symptoms at all and are unaware that they have been infected.

Most cases of hep B are acute, lasting less than six months and resulting in total recovery. However, 10 percent of the people who contract the virus become carriers of hepatitis B, infecting others with whom they come into contact. And 90 percent of infected children under age five and 5 to 10 percent of infected people over age five will develop chronic hepatitis,

Children under five are at special risk for chronic hep.

increasing their risk for developing liver problems—usually many years, even decades, after infection. An estimated 4,000 to 5,000 people die every year from liver disease caused by HBV.

The hep B virus is found in infected blood and body fluids, and is mainly spread through sharing needles, typically during IV drug use, or through sexual contact with an infected person. Mothers also can pass on HBV to their babies at birth. Other, less common means for transmission of the virus include contact with unsterilized contaminated surgical or dental tools, accidental punctures with infected needles or razors, or use of infected instruments during acupuncture, tattooing, ear or body part piercing, or manicures.

As a junior in high school, Trish was an active participant in after-school sports and extracurricular activities. She was always on the go and managed to pull off straight As as well. After missing two weeks of classes with a severe case of fatigue and low-grade fever, Trish went to her HMO for a physical. It just wasn't like her to be dragging around.

When the doctor informed her that she had hepatitis B, Trish was shocked. She had heard hep was a disease that only druggies and prostitutes could catch, not A-students who rarely went to parties! Trish told the doctor that she had never used drugs or alcohol and was not sexually active. How could she have hep?

While attending a support group meeting for people with hepatitis in the city where she lived, Trish became curious when another girl mentioned that she had gotten a butterfly tattooed on her shoulder at a rather grungy parlor, and she suspected the needles used there as the source of her illness.

Trish, too, had been tattooed (on her hip, with a small red rose) only a few months before her illness began. After the meeting, Trish approached the other girl and compared notes. Both had been tattooed at the same location, and they realized that this was probably the source of their hepatitis B infections.

Trish's symptoms eventually subsided, but she does not know yet if she is a carrier or whether

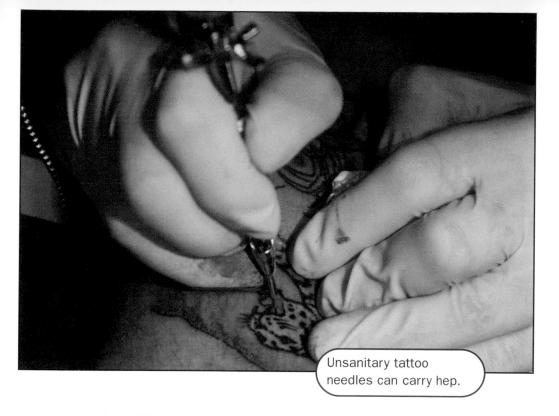

Unsanitary tattoo needles can carry hep.

she will develop liver problems as an adult. Just knowing that she may harbor the hep virus in her body has changed Trish as a person, transforming her from an active go-getter to a more quiet and introspective individual, with life-and-death concerns weighing on her mind.

Avoiding HBV

If you come into contact with even small amounts of infected blood, the hepatitis B virus can invade your body by entering your bloodstream through a cut or puncture in your skin or through the mucous membranes. Thus, HBV is spread the same way as AIDS—but it is 100 times more contagious than AIDS.

According to the Centers for Disease Control and Prevention (CDC) in Atlanta, 55 percent of cases of hepatitis B are contracted through sexual contact—41 percent via heterosexual activity and 14 percent from homosexual activity. Another 12 percent acquire HBV through sharing needles, 4 percent from household contact with an infected person, 2 percent during employment in the health care field, and 1 percent in the other known ways; the remaining 26 percent of hepatitis B cases are contracted in unknown ways.

Since the virus can survive on a dry surface for a week or longer, many people have no idea that they have come into contact with an infectious agent. And, since most carriers do not realize that they are infectious, they continue to unknowingly pass on the virus to friends, loved ones, even casual acquaintances. "I think many people whose infections can't be traced are getting it either sexually or through living in a household with a carrier who hasn't been identified," says Dr. Miriam Alter of the CDC. "All you need is a minute amount of blood getting into your bloodstream, say by brushing your teeth with an infected person's brush or using the same razor."

Health professionals are especially concerned about sexually active teens and young adults who may not be aware of the substantial risk of contracting HBV through sexual contact. And, since the use of heroin and other injectable drugs is currently on the rise

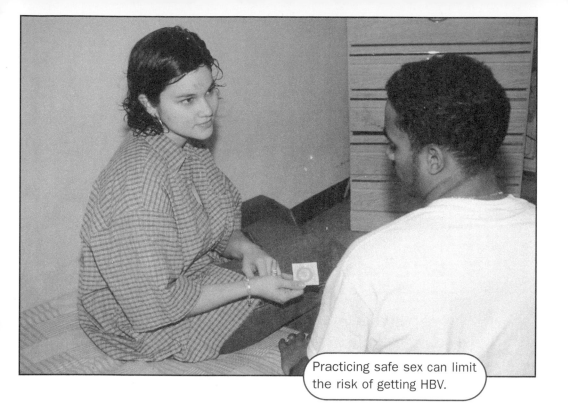

Practicing safe sex can limit the risk of getting HBV.

among young people, health authorities are expecting a correlating increase in cases of hepatitis B. From age twenty to twenty-nine is considered the peak risk period, and males are much more likely to come down with the disease after exposure to HBV.

Since treatment for hepatitis B is expensive and not always effective, prevention is the best plan of action. Practicing safe sex and avoiding drugs and drug abusers can dramatically reduce your chances for developing the disease. There is also an HBV vaccine available, which is currently recommended for virtually everyone: Newborns can be vaccinated, as can school children and teenagers. (More on prevention in chapter five.)

Hep Invader C

People at risk for contracting HBV are also at risk for HCV, another blood-borne hepatitis virus. In the U.S., approximately 150,000 people are infected with hepatitis C every year. Only 30 to 40 percent of people who contract HCV will experience symptoms after they are exposed to the virus, but most will eventually develop chronic hepatitis and become lifelong carriers of the disease. In this country, 8,000 to 10,000 people die every year from HCV-related chronic liver disease.

Hepatitis C is mainly spread through contaminated needles. Blood transfusions given before 1990—when screening methods were instituted to eliminate contaminated blood supplies—have helped to spread HCV as well. According to the CDC, 40 percent of infections with HCV are due to needle sharing by IV drug users, 5 percent occur in health care workers, and 2 percent are from blood transfusions; the causes of the remaining 53 percent of cases of HCV are unknown.

Sexual activity is not a major cause for the spread of HCV but, since there are an estimated 3.5 million chronic carriers of hepatitis C in the U.S., sexual behavior is believed to account for a significant portion of the new infections which occur in this country.

After a routine physical, Cole, a twenty-five-year-old nutritionist at a major metropolitan hospital, was informed that his liver enzymes were elevated, an indication that something was amiss. Since Cole felt fine, he ignored the test results—for ten years. Then, during another routine physical, Cole was diagnosed with hepatitis C. For the previous decade, he realized in horror, he had been an unaware HCV carrier! And he had consumed moderate amounts of alcohol, which probably was unwise, since his liver had been compromised by the presence of the chronic infection.

Cole has found it difficult to tell others about his illness, which he does not know how he got and which makes him suffer from debilitating bouts of fatigue. Single, Cole admits that having hepatitis is "uncomfortable from a sexual standpoint, especially talking about it with a potential sexual partner." But Cole also realizes that his disease could be a lot worse. "AIDS has put things in perspective for people with hepatitis," he says. "We're not dying as fast."

Hep D—A Less Common Invader

Hepatitis D is not yet a reportable disease, that is, it is not routinely recorded in public health records. This makes the exact incidence of the hepatitis D virus unknown. However, the CDC estimates that there may be as many as 13,000 new HDV infections annually in the United States. And HDV is much more common in other parts of the world. The virus is widespread in South America, Africa, the Middle East, and Italy.

Hepatitis D occurs only in those infected with hepatitis B because the D virus requires HBV in order to reproduce itself. In this country, hep D is most often diagnosed in IV drug abusers, who will sometimes suffer from a severe case of acute or chronic HBV-HDV. People who have received multiple blood transfusions may also develop a co-infection of HBV-HDV.

Hepatitis can kill: Although you probably will not die from it right away, hepatitis B, C, and D can lead to cirrhosis or severe scarring of the liver, liver cancer, and other fatal illnesses. There is no vaccine for hepatitis C or D, but immunity to hepatitis B will prevent a co-infection with HDV. If you have not been vaccinated and you discover that you have been exposed to hepatitis B, an immediate dose of immune globulin (Ig) may help to prevent infection.

Of course, the best option is to prevent exposure to hepatitis in the first place—by practicing safe sex and avoiding drug use and drug users. However, since a significant number of cases of the hepatitis virus are caused by unknown factors, the grim reality is that you may not be able to protect yourself 100 percent. That is why it is important to recognize the symptoms of hepatitis—and to know what to do if you think you might have hep.

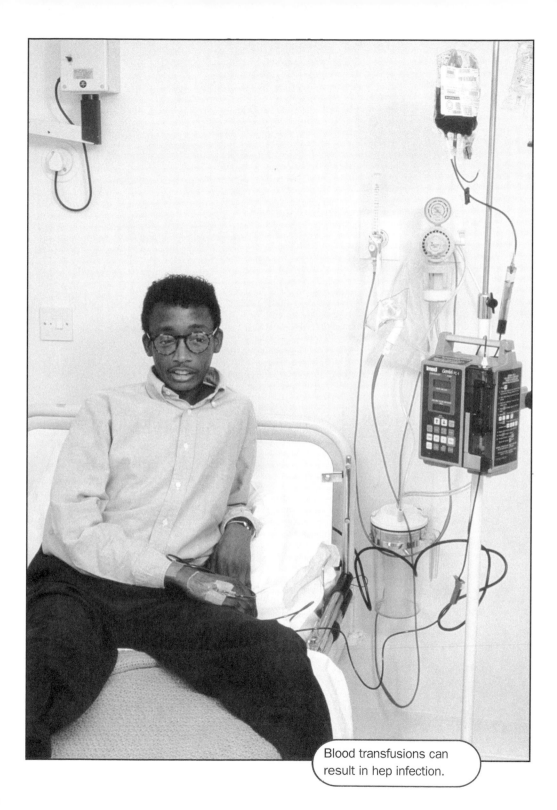
Blood transfusions can result in hep infection.

Chapter Four

Diagnosis and Treatment

Nearly 5 million Americans are chronically infected with hepatitis, most with the viruses HBV and HCV. Approximately 15,000 die each year from complications of the disease. So far, there is no cure.

Not much is known about the hep viruses most recently identified: HFV, HGV, and its HGBV variants. Only one confirmed case of hepatitis F has been recorded in Canada, for example, where it is categorized as a rare illness distinct from the other hepatitis viruses. Hepatitis G and GB are believed to be blood-borne strains of the hep virus, but researchers think they may be like HDV in that they seem to occur only as co-infections in people who already suffer from hepatitis—typically HCV. Medical researchers suspect that other, as yet undiscovered hepatitis viruses also exist.

Diagnosing Hep

There are two main reasons for suspecting you may have hepatitis:

• You are suffering from mild to severe symptoms (as listed below); and/or

• You believe that you have been exposed to the virus or to a potential carrier of the virus.

The following are common symptoms of hepatitis: flu-like illness; nausea, vomiting, or diarrhea; decrease in appetite or weight loss; mild fever; weakness or fatigue; muscle or joint aches; abdominal pain; jaundice; dark urine; and light clay-colored stools.

If you have traveled to developing countries or used IV drugs, are employed in a day care or health care setting, or have a loved one or sexual partner who has hepatitis, you might want to be tested for the virus, even if you do not have any symptoms and feel fine.

Hepatitis is not easy to diagnose. For young people, the symptoms may resemble mononucleosis ("the kissing disease") and can be mistaken for this common teenage illness. Hep is readily misdiagnosed as a case of the flu or completely overlooked when no symptoms occur. If a patient complains of dark urine or has the obvious signs of jaundice, however, hepatitis is easier for a physician to spot.

Blood tests are used to diagnose hep. Screening the

levels of liver enzymes in your blood can indicate whether this organ is functioning properly. The blood can also be tested for the presence of antibodies to the most prevalent hepatitis viruses—A, B, C, and D. These tests can determine whether you are acutely ill, suffering from a chronic infection, or in the process of recovering from hep. Blood tests will also indicate whether you have developed immunity to the prevailing hep viruses.

For the other, less common hep viruses, accurate blood screening tests are not yet commercially available. Sometimes HEV is diagnosed by testing stool (feces) samples for the virus. There are no such tests for HFV, HGV, and HGBV.

Follow-up tests are important if you are diagnosed with HBV or HCV. Blood tests should be repeated after three months, and again in six months, after the initial diagnosis is made, in order to determine whether you may be a carrier of the virus. Routine testing is also recommended for pregnant women since up to 90 percent of the babies born to infected women also develop hepatitis.

Treating Hep

A diagnosis of hepatitis is not a death sentence. In most instances of HAV and HEV, and in many acute cases of HBV, the virus simply runs its course and the liver recuperates on its own. All you need to do is rest—

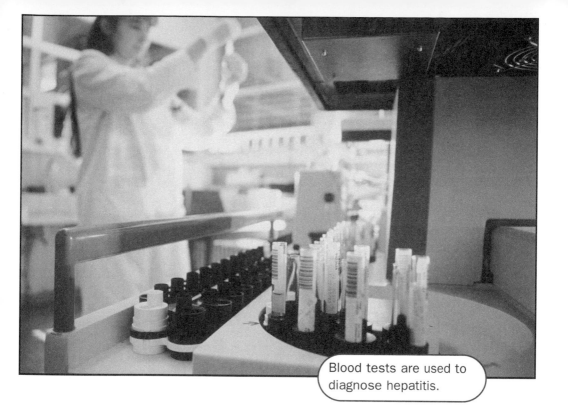

Blood tests are used to diagnose hepatitis.

which is easy if you have symptoms and feel terrible, but which can prove to be a challenge if you are asymptomatic. In either case, rest is imperative.

An easy-to-digest low-fat diet can prove helpful if you are suffering from nausea, vomiting, diarrhea, and/or appetite loss. This means eliminating all fried foods, fast foods, and rich desserts until your symptoms go away (which is a healthier way to eat anyway). Strenuous exercise is not a good idea until your doctor says it is okay to resume your normal physical activities. Of course, alcohol and caffeine are to be avoided, as are all recreational drugs and most medications. Your doctor can advise you on the use of any prescription medications you might be taking.

For those who develop chronic hepatitis—typically as HCV, more rarely as HBV—there is primarily one drug treatment prescribed in the United States: Alpha interferon, an injectable drug course used for a six-month period, can boost the body's immune response, reducing inflammation in the livers of hep sufferers. But interferon itself causes serious side effects—including depression, hair loss, a reduction in disease-fighting white blood cells, and a worsening of the symptoms of hepatitis. Also, interferon is effective in only 25 to 35 percent of users. Often, the virus dies down during the treatment, only to reoccur once the drug therapy is halted. Treatment with interferon is expensive, oftentimes proving prohibitive for those without adequate medical insurance.

In the most serious cases of chronic hepatitis, a liver transplant may be recommended. The liver can function until it is almost two-thirds destroyed before this hardy organ begins to fail. But when the liver fails, you will die unless you receive a healthy transplanted organ.

Liver transplant is an extremely expensive and risky procedure. In some cases, the hepatitis virus still circulating in the blood after the damaged liver is removed rapidly infects the new organ. Obviously, there is no guaranteed cure for hepatitis.

When Naomi Judd was told by a doctor that she had only a few years to live, she responded with a strong urge to prove him wrong. "I could not wait to get out of his office," she told the *Saturday Evening Post* some six years later. "I mean, the negativity, I could taste it. From the beginning, I knew that approach was doomed to failure." She also experienced a very negative response to the six-month course of interferon that had been prescribed.

Naomi decided to create her own cure for her disease: a positive approach to her illness accomplished through self-healing. That is why, before retiring to her farm in Franklin, Tennessee, Naomi took The Judds on their now-famous year-long Farewell Tour across the U.S.

As a former nurse, Naomi knew how her body worked. She also knew that "medicine is not God." Instead, Naomi believed in the power of love: She felt that the positive interaction with her fans, the excitement and joy of performing before massive, appreciative audiences, would cure her by helping to boost her body's immune reaction to the virus that had invaded her liver. "I knew I had to stimulate my beleaguered immune system, and that I could jumpstart my system and get juiced," she explained. "One person in a million has the privilege of standing on the stage during an ovation—and feeling that electricity . . . Music and love are just direct access, you know?"

Naomi combined this unique healing concept with daily "quiet time" spent meditating, praying, reading spiritual books, and listening to relaxing music. She cut out junk food and coffee, learned to do biofeedback, and began to spend more time outside in nature. Private, nonworking "family days" became a fun, relaxing, and sacred routine for Naomi, her two daughters, and her husband.

These days, Naomi Judd continues to try to live what she calls a "soulful life." "Even though they're saying this is a no-win disease, I'm going for the cure," she says of her hepatitis—which has now been in remission for more than eight years.

What You Need to Know

Naomi Judd is an inspirational example of someone who has transformed a hepatitis diagnosis into a reason for changing her life—for the better. Sometimes, disease can serve as a spiritual wake-up call, a motivating means for overhauling an unhealthy or risky lifestyle and adjusting one's outlook on life.

But why wait until you contract this or any other illness before stopping to take note of self-destructive behaviors and beginning to pay attention to the quality of your life? By making some relatively simple changes now, you may never have to listen to these life-changing words: "Welcome to hepatitis. You are very infectious."

Sometimes disease can act as a spiritual wake-up call.

Chapter Five

Preventing Hepatitis

*W*hen Gerome's girlfriend told him she needed to talk, he freaked out, fearing that she might be pregnant. But Sasha gave him an even bigger shock: She had hepatitis B, which she had caught from her previous boyfriend, a heroin addict.

Gerome immediately made an appointment at the neighborhood health clinic. He felt okay, but he was scared stiff. He didn't know much about the disease, but he was pretty sure you could catch it if you didn't practice safe sex. Embarrassed but proud of himself, Gerome told the nurse that he and Sasha had always used condoms.

Waiting for the test results was an agonizing experience, one Gerome vowed he would never go through again. The blood test turned out

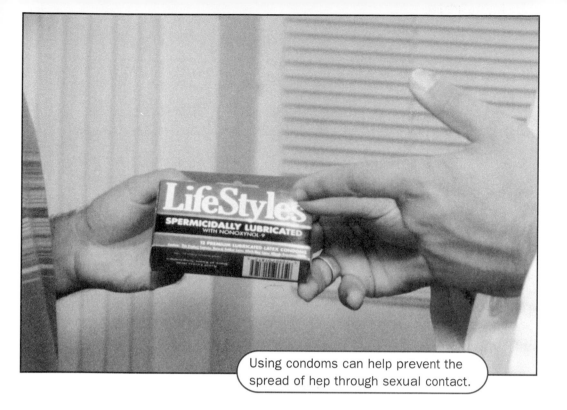

Using condoms can help prevent the spread of hep through sexual contact.

negative for hep, but the doctor advised Gerome to get vaccinated. Gerome readily agreed, and he gratefully accepted the sample packet of condoms offered by the nurse.

Vaccines

"With increased awareness, hepatitis B could be totally preventable one day," says liver specialist Dr. David A. Shafritz. "If widespread vaccination programs can be implemented—such as the ones that eliminated polio—this disease can be eliminated too."

The vaccine for hepatitis B is readily available at doctors' offices and health clinics, and the triple-dose immunization is effective for at least ten years. The

Centers for Disease Control and Prevention recommends routine immunization for infants and for school children in around the sixth grade, with "catch up" vaccines for nonimmunized teens and young adults. For those with high-risk lifestyles, such as drug abusers and people with multiple sex partners, public health authorities advise immediate vaccination. For people working in the health care industry, the vaccine is widely available at no charge to those employees with jobs that expose them to infectious material such as blood or blood products. The HBV vaccine will also prevent an HBV-HDV co-infection.

There are two vaccines available in the U.S. for hepatitis A, but the exact period of effectiveness is unknown. The CDC recommends this vaccine only for those who are most at risk—such as travelers to the Third World and, possibly, children over age two who are in day care.

If a nonimmunized person who is exposed to HBV or HAV is able to quickly obtain a one-time dose of immune globulin—before symptoms appear—infection may be prevented. There is no vaccine for HCV, HEV, or for the less common viruses HDV, HGV, and HGBV.

There are ways you can help to protect yourself against all of the hep viruses. By adopting certain behaviors and refraining from others, you can greatly reduce your chances for developing hepatitis. The following lists provide practical advice for those who wish to be safe from hepatitis—rather than very, very sorry.

To Avoid HAV:

- Wash your hands before eating or handling food.

- Wash your hands after using the bathroom or changing a baby's diaper.

- Do not eat uncooked shellfish such as raw oysters or clams.

- Wash all raw fruits and vegetables thoroughly.

- Avoid restaurants that seem unsanitary.

To Avoid HBV, HCV, and HDV:

- Always practice safe sex.

- Do not use IV drugs.

- Never share needles.

- Do not share razors, toothbrushes, nail clippers, or any other item that may come into contact with someone else's blood.

- Make sure that instruments are sterile if you get a tattoo or have a body part pierced.

- Frequent only trustworthy acupuncture practitioners, manicurists, and dental and medical offices.

To Avoid HEV:

- Drink only boiled or bottled water whenever traveling in foreign countries (and no ice cubes!).

- Never eat uncooked shellfish, or raw fruits or vegetables when visiting underdeveloped countries.

- Do not swim or bathe in water you suspect may be contaminated.

By protecting yourself against hepatitis A through E, it is likely that you will avoid contracting hepatitis F, G, GB, or any of the as yet unidentified hep viruses. (If you have to receive blood, however, your chances do increase for contracting these newer viruses, which are still unable to be screened from donated blood supplies.) To protect your liver from toxic, nonviral hepatitis as well, be sure to do the following:

- Drink alcohol only in moderation, if at all.

- Avoid recreational drug use.

- Avoid prolonged use of medications linked to liver disease (such as acetaminophen, disulfiram, or isoniazid).

- Take care when using herbal remedies, as certain herbs can be toxic to the liver (e.g., chaparral, comfrey, germander).

If you have a drug problem, seek a support group or other type of help.

Hep and Society

Since the mid-1960s, hepatitis has become a major world health problem. With as many as 500 million people around the globe currently believed to be hep carriers, medical researchers predict that they are just beginning to see the long-term consequences of infections contracted over the past three and a half decades: severe liver disorders, end-stage liver disease, and liver cancer. People who experimented with injectable drugs during the free-wheeling '60s, for example, before hepatitis C was even identified, are just now reaching the age when the resulting liver damage is becoming a serious threat. The incidence of liver cancer has risen by at least 55 percent since 1984, and medical authorities attribute this increase to the widespread viral forms of hepatitis.

Researchers are experimenting with an array of antiviral drugs for future use with hepatitis, including one government-approved medication that appears to reduce liver inflammation in adults with chronic HBV. It is hoped that the vaccine for HBV will serve to eliminate this form of the virus in the next generation. In the meantime, you know everything you need to in order to protect yourself against hepatitis—or to obtain treatment if you suspect you may have hep. Now it is up to you to do so.

Glossary

active hepatitis   A hepatitis infection that causes symptoms in the body.

acute hepatitis   A short-term hepatitis infection, which lasts six months or less.

AIDS   Acquired immune deficiency syndrome, a serious viral disease most commonly transmitted through needle sharing or sexual contact with infected persons.

alpha interferon   An antiviral drug that boosts the body's immune response to fight off certain viruses; used to treat HBV and HCV infections.

antibodies   Proteins produced by the body in response to foreign substances as part of the immune system's natural defense against viruses, bacteria, and other invaders.

biofeedback   A form of psychological conditioning used to teach the body how to control automatic functions such as blood pressure and breathing; various techniques can be learned in order to help ease pain and reduce or eliminate the symptoms of certain illnesses.

blood plasma   The fluid portion of the blood; it can be dried and stored for use in blood donation.

blood transfusion   The use of donated blood supplies in order to replenish depleted stores in cases of accidents, surgical or birthing losses, or illnesses that cause severe blood loss.

carrier   Anyone who is infected with a contagious disease that can be transmitted to others. The person may not have any symptoms or know that the disease is present.

chronic hepatitis   A long-lasting or lifelong hepatitis infection with or without symptoms.

cirrhosis   Degeneration of the liver with scarring and inflammation.

disulfiram   The medication commonly prescribed to aid in alcohol withdrawal (brand name Antabuse).

enzyme   A substance that causes or speeds up chemical reactions; in the body, enzymes aid in digestion and other essential functions.

epidemic   An outbreak of a contagious disease that spreads rapidly, causing a great number of cases in a community or country.

hepatitis   Inflammation of the liver.

immune globulin (Ig)   A blood product derived from donors that has antibody activity, so it can be used to boost the immune system function of recipients.

immune system   The body's natural defense system which battles against foreign invaders such as bacteria and viruses.

immunity   The body's ability to fight off or resist disease.

isoniazid   An antibacterial prescription medication used in the treatment of the infectious lung disease tuberculosis (brand names Laniazid and Nydrazid).

jaundice   A distinct yellowing of the skin and the whites of the eyes due to a buildup in the bloodstream of a yellow-orange substance produced by the liver.

liver   A large gland located in the upper right portion of the abdomen which is responsible for many important body functions, including the digestion of food and the detoxification of harmful substances, such as alcohol and drugs.

liver transplant   A surgical operation to replace a diseased liver with a healthy donated organ.

mononucleosis   An acute, infectious viral disease causing sore throat, fatigue, and flu-like symptoms; it primarily occurs in children and young adults.

mucous membranes   Mucus-secreting areas lining
the body's openings such as the nostrils, anus,
and vagina.

polio   A serious contagious viral disease that causes
paralysis; use of vaccines has greatly reduced its
incidence in the U.S.

toxic hepatitis   Liver disease caused by prolonged
exposure to damaging chemicals, such as alcohol,
drugs, and other substances poisonous to the liver.

viral hepatitis   Contagious diseases of the liver
caused by at least five different viruses, including
HAV, HBV, HCV, HDV, and HEV.

virus   An invisible infectious agent that is smaller
than bacteria and requires a host (such as cells in
the human body) to reproduce and thrive; it may
remain in the body in an inactive state for long
periods of time before damaging cells. Viral diseases include the common cold, influenza (or flu),
chicken pox, measles, mumps, and certain forms
of hepatitis.

Where to Go for Help

American Liver Foundation
75 Maiden Lane, Suite 603
New York, NY 10038
(800) 223-0179
Web site: http://www.liverfoundation.org

Centers for Disease Control and Prevention
National Center for Infectious Diseases
Hepatitis Branch
1600 Clifton Road NE
Atlanta, GA 30333
(888) 443-7232
Web site: http://www.cdc.gov

Center for Liver Diseases
University of Miami
1500 NW 12th Avenue, Suite 1101
Miami, FL 33136
(305) 243-5787

Hepatitis B Coalition
1573 Selby Avenue
St. Paul, MN 55104
(651) 647-9009
Web site: http://www.immunize.org

Hepatitis B Foundation
700 East Butler Avenue
Doyletown, PA 18901-2697
(215) 489-4900
Web site: http://www.hepb.org

Hepatitis C Foundation
(215) 672-2606
Web site: http://www.hepcfoundation.org

Hepatitis Foundation International
30 Sunrise Terrace
Cedar Grove, NJ 07009
(800) 891-0707
Web site: http://www.HepFI.org

National Association of Alcohol and Drug Abuse
Counselors
3717 Columbia Pike, Suite 300
Arlington, VA 22204
(800) 548-0497

National Heart, Lung, and Blood Institute
National Institutes of Health
Building 31, Room 4A-21
9000 Rockville Pike
Bethesda, MD 20892
(301) 592-8573

Youth Crisis Hotline
(800) 448-4663

For Further Reading

Everson, Gregory T. *Living with Hepatitis C: A Survivor's Guide.* New York: Hatherleigh Press, 1998.

Judd, Naomi, and Bud Schaetzle. *Love Can Build a Bridge.* New York: Villard Books, 1993.

Levine, Arnold J. *Viruses.* New York: Scientific American Library, 1992.

McKoy, Kathy, and Charles Wibbelsman. *Life Happens: A Teenager's Guide to Friends, Failure, Sexuality, Love . . .* New York: Berkeley Publishing, 1996.

Roybal, Beth Ann Petro. *Hepatitis C: A Personal Guide to Good Health.* Berkeley, CA: Ulysses Press, 1997.

Salter, Charles A. *Food Risks and Controversies.* Brookfield, CT: Millbrook Press, 1993.

Schoon, Douglas D. *HIV-AIDS and Hepatitis: Everything You Need to Know to Protect Yourself and Others.* Albany, NY: Milady Publications, 1993.

Shader, Laurel and Jon Zondervan. *Mononucleosis and Other Infectious Diseases.* New York: Chelsea House Publishers, 1989.

Silverstein, Alvin, Virginia Silverstein, and Robert Silverstein. *Hepatitis.* Hillside, NJ: Enslow Publishers, 1994.

Woods, Samuel G. *Everything You Need to Know About Sexually Transmitted Disease.* Rev. ed. New York: Rosen Publishing Group, 1997.

Index

About the Author

Virginia Aronson is a health writer and author of more than twenty books, including books for young adults. She lives in South Florida with her writer husband and young son.

Photo Credits

Cover and pp 24 and 47 by Brian Silak; pp 2, 6 by Ira Fox; pp 9, 14, 29, 37, 51 © Custom Medical; pp 12 © CORBIS; pp 17 by Ethan Zindler; pp 19 by Maike Schulz; pp 23, 31, 41 © Superstock; pp 33 by Ira Fox; pp 45 © DPA/The Image Works.

Series Design
Annie O'Donnell

Layout
Rebecca Stern